# The Man Who Killed The Equal Sign

## 150 Quotations, Questions, and Abstractions

Alexander Ngu

Amaya Odilon Ngu

Amaya Odilon Kosso

The Man Who Killed The Equal Sign

# DEDICATION

This book is dedicated to the Kosso & Ngu Families of the
land currently known as Cameroon, Africa.
Special Thanks to Mr. Marcos Ralston Elliott.

# ACKNOWLEDGMENTS

Thank you to my Family

Thank you to my Teachers

Thank you to my Readers

# DISCLAIMER

This book is an artistic exploration not meant to conform to any specific genre. Proceed with an open mind.

The Man Who Killed The Equal Sign

# CONTENTS

The Man Who Killed The Equal Sign

# I

## EPIGRAPH

The death of the equal sign defines the birth of a new civilization

- The Man Who Killed The Equal Sign

We cannot solve infinitely complex problems with finite solutions

Amaya Odilon Kosso | Alexander Ngu

# II

## AUTHOR'S NOTE

The goal of this book is to communicate my ideas concisely and understandably. To accomplish this goal, I have chosen to include only the most essential quotes, questions, and abstract concepts from my notes compiled over the past few years.

Each quote in this book has been carefully considered. I won't bore you with lengthy explanations, and I don't anticipate your complete agreement with each quote. Also, note that some quotes are justified in other quotes. Something from this book inspires you to think more about the world around you.
If you have any questions or need clarification, feel free to reach out via email at tmwktes@gmail.com

# III

## PREFACE

Greetings, I am Amaya Odilon Kosso also known as Alexander Ngu also known as Amaya Odilon Ngu, I was born in Yaoundé, Cameroon. I am honored to introduce myself as the son of Emmanuel Soninga Kosso and the grandson of Bah David Ngu. My paternal roots belong to the Gbaya (Baya) tribe, originating from the Eastern region of Cameroon in Bertoua, while my maternal roots belong to the Mbu Baforchu tribe in the western region of Cameroon. In future works, I will delve into more details about my personal life, giving you a chance to learn more about me.

From a young age, I was fascinated with the concept of intelligence, and this interest only grew as I grew older. I spent many years obsessed with the question, "What is intelligence?" but was not satisfied with any of the definitions that I came across as they were either incomplete or restricted to a specific domain such as biological or computational intelligence. My present endeavors revolve around the concept of unified intelligence, which posits that intelligence manifests itself in various forms. I aim to unravel the fundamental intelligence that serves as the foundation for all intelligent systems, regardless of their form or function.

To my surprise, I found that very few people had pondered the question at hand. I considered this a remarkable observation because to me it was the most significant question one could pose. If we were able to unravel the mysteries of intelligence, we could unveil the underlying language or code of nature. This would enable us to tackle a multitude of issues that plague humanity. Consequently, I took it upon myself to define intelligence and in doing so, made a breakthrough that I am confident will alter the course of humanity.

I have a suspicion that our use of numbers constrains our comprehension of reality, and we should employ alternative symbols to express ideas. While mathematics serves as the foundation for modern science, it has been demonstrated to be an incomplete knowledge system, implying that other derivative systems of knowledge are also incomplete.

In my opinion, the present definition of intelligence and its association with memory and problem-solving is also incomplete. I conjecture that intelligence does not reside solely in the physical brain but is omnipresent throughout nature. To fully comprehend the mysteries of nature and establish a comprehensive and coherent definition of intelligence, we must discover a language that is consistent across all systems and scales. This is crucial in unifying physical, biological, chemical, computational, and other systems. In essence, we must tackle a question that has confounded scholars for centuries: What are the Laws of Nature?

My instinct tells me that to achieve this objective, we need to discover a universal language that is applicable at all scales. This language must be comprehensive enough to remain consistent at both the infinitesimal and finite levels and thus must possess infinite generality. Unfortunately, our current knowledge systems, including mathematics, are insufficient for this task. I believe that our use of numbers and the equal sign hinders our ability to obtain a complete and coherent understanding of natural systems. While the language of mathematics serves as the foundation for many of our current civilization's systems, it also results in incomplete mathematically based systems that contain inherent points of failure. These failures are prevalent in our computational, economic, and social systems, and are attributed to fundamental inadequacies, inconsistencies, and eventual decay within these systems. My intuition guides me to the conclusion that to avoid such a fate, we must transcend the limitations of mathematics and adopt a more comprehensive and coherent language.

My contribution is significant because I have introduced a new language that surpasses Mathematics and enables us to represent the interplay of diverse systems at every level. I refer to it as "The Language of Intelligence" since it accounts for the interaction of all intelligent systems, whether physical or non-physical. I contend that this language is the key to defining nature itself. My name is Alexander Amaya Odilon Ngu Kosso, but people often call me "The Man Who Killed the Equal Sign" since the language I discovered eliminates the need for an equal sign in most representations. This new language is applicable to every domain and scale. In this book, I have employed short quotations and abstractions to express the language's relevance. These quotations and abstractions align with the language of intelligence and the equation of Intelligence, which I outline in the book's final pages. They are not presented in any specific order. For a more comprehensive academic defense of the equation of Intelligence and the language of intelligence, please refer to my papers "Dimensional Complexity and Algorithmic Efficiency" and "The Language of Intelligence." A way to access these documents is provided in the resources section of this book.

My instinct tells me this novel framework will provide humanity with a universal truth or agreement, resulting in novel problem-solving approaches. As such, I authored "The Man Who Killed The Equal Sign" as a compilation of easy-to-digest quotations, questions, and abstractions culled from a few years of my notes. This book offers insight into my thoughts on my journey to discovery.

# IV

## QUOTATIONS, QUESTIONS & ABSTRACTIONS

# Who am I, where am I going, And how would I get there?

I am present.

My name is Amaya Odilon
Kosso also known as
Alexander Ngu. I am the man
who killed the equal = sign.

# It's a New Age

The old Alexander hath conquered the world with destruction. The New Alexander shall water the world with creation.

# The last war is fought for the unveiling of Truth.

Truth does not need citation.
Truth is the foundation.

Truth is complete. The lies are incomplete.

Education is the journey to

uncover the Truth.

A lack of understanding is not indicative of a lack of truth.

# Truth precedes Proof.

If man's journey is to search

for truth, what happens when

said truth is discovered?

All men are born with The

Power of Self-Definition.

# The Power to Define is the greatest power a man can exercise.

We must gain awareness of Truth and acknowledge it, to re-calibrate man's relationship with nature.

Ideas > Symbols > Quotes > Books.

Ideas > Matter.

Imaginary > Real.

# Symbols are discrete representations of continuous ideas.

Simplicity is key to demystifying nature.

How can a man call himself intelligent when he has yet to define Intelligence itself?

A symbolic abstraction is the simplest and most digestible representation of an idea.

# Abstraction is key to Generalization.

# Abstraction is key to demystifying complexity

A symbolic abstraction is digestible by a young child and an old man.

# Intelligence is the formalization of generality.

# Generalization is key to intelligence.

# The Representation Precedes the Interpretation

# The Representation
# >
# The Interpretation

# What is Intelligence?

# What are intelligent systems?

# How do intelligent systems

# interact?

What is the distinction between General Intelligence, Nature's Intelligence, and Artificial Intelligence? and how do we reconcile all three?

Abstraction is the key to Generalization.
Generalization is the key to intelligence.
Intelligence is the key to information.
Information is the key to free energy.
Free Energy is the key to a Utopia.

# Is Intelligence local to the physical brain or is it an emergent phenomenon?

# How do we explain the emergence, interaction, and evolution of natural systems?

# Creativity is indicative of intelligence

At the edge of reality,
intelligence is an abstraction.

Intelligence is the algorithm
that underpins all phenomena.

.

# Intelligence has a closer relationship with perceptibility than with memory and problem-solving

# Intelligence is the mother of energy.

Intelligence > Energy.

.

# Emergent systems experience birth and death

If our mathematics is in itself incomplete, then all derivative knowledge systems will also be incomplete.

Equality is an incomplete
representation of the
fundamental relationship
between natural phenomena.

The equal sign  = is the root
of modern man's problems.

# Denotation does not mean equality.

Generality

>

Equality.

# Truth is Symbolic.

# What is the simplest representation of language?

# What is the language of Nature and the Nature of language?

Intelligence is omnipresent.

# Language constraints Truth.

The Emergence of human language is indicative of regression, not the progression of intelligence.

Emergence-creation is
progressive and
Evolution-dying is regressive.

Creation precedes
Destruction.

Evolution is incomplete
without reconciliation with
creation.

The death of the equal sign

=

defines the birth of a new

civilization

# Welcome to the Age of

# Intelligence.

In the beginning,

I had a triangle, an infinity,

And a circle.

In the beginning,

there was emergence,

interaction, and evolution.

All systems Dance.

All Systems have a Unique

Dance.

All Systems have a Unique

dance that all Systems

Understand.

Sensitivity is inversely
proportional to
dimensionality.

Interpolation requires assumptions. This is a limitation.

Evolution is the finitary
expression of intelligence.

Infinitely complex problems cannot be solved with finitary solutions.

# The only problem left to solve is Complexity.

Intelligence cannot be created or replicated. It can only be discovered and accessed.

# Dancing with Complexity.

Darkness precedes light.

# Interaction requires consensus

Your theory is incomplete if it crumbles under infinite circumstances.

# Philosophers are architects of the imaginary.

Size gives a man a false sense
of individuality.

Man is a triangle. Woman is a circle.

Randomness is the pattern of
Generalization.

# The point of emergence is the anchor for all systems.

No finite set of axioms can completely define an infinite system.

The = sign is finite and
incomplete and
The ∞ is infinite and
complete.

Pre-emergent phenomena are
unbounded.

# Post-emergent phenomena are bounded.

This is beyond mathematics,
this is about Truth.

The infinity symbols give us a complete interpretation of natural interaction.

How does a system fit within
the Universality of all systems?

I just submitted my
dissertation
to Nature.

Scarcity is a man-made
phenomenon.

Planned obsolescence is an
implementation of faux
scarcity.

Mathematics is an elevator to
the infinite
floors of philosophy.

To solve the problems of
humanity,
we must go beyond
mathematics.

Usefulness is overrated.

Intuition > Information.

The Queen must have the genetic potential to birth her entire civilization.

A boy becomes a man when
he becomes aware of Truth
and acknowledges it as such.

If all physical phenomena is emergent, then the imaginary precedes the real.

I have a beef with the equal sign =.

Imagination dances best with novelty.

Scarcity is overrated.

Value must be divorced from Scarcity and married to Abundance.

# What is nature's currency?

What is the single most valuable thing we can imagine?

# Numbers always Lie.

No amount of acquired
knowledge can surpass Truth.

The goal is not to own everything. The goal is to share everything.

Mathematics cannot model
nature in its totality.

Thoughts are triangular and
emotions are circular.

If the stability and growth of a system are built on the limitation of the stability and growth of another system, then that system is oppressive.

# What is nature's consensus algorithm?

The economic consensus mechanism must be immutable,  incorruptible, and unownable.

Truth is the only consensus
mechanism that eliminates
exploitation.

Emancipation is the action taken upon awareness and acknowledgment of Truth.

Uncertainty is a tool for
architecting reality.

# Fulfillment > Happiness

Love is meaningless without
hate.

The greatness of a civilization is not measured by the height of its buildings but by the cohesion of its systems.

The Intelligence standard is a way of evaluating the completeness and consistency of a system, to account for interoperability with other systems in its environment.

# The Language of Intelligence

# defines the interaction of

# intelligent systems.

Proof-of-Intelligence is the consensus mechanism used to validate interactions between intelligent systems

Demystifying complexity is
akin to demystifying nature
and the universe.

Computationally bounded
systems are fundamentally
incomplete and corruptible.

Energy is an incomplete representation of infinite phenomena.

Our consensus algorithm
must not be bounded in a
computational representation.

Man-made algorithms are
filters that distort not just the
perception of reality but
reality itself.

The validation of any contract must be made between man and nature, not between man and machine.

Whoever writes the algorithm
controls the interactions.

# Algorithmic Apartheid.

# Death is the Climax of Inefficiency.

The veneration of the origin is key to maintaining connection, sustaining growth, and delaying extinction.

# The arrogance of Data.

# Dimensional Complexity
# &
# Algorithmic Efficiency.

# Science is Dead

Discretization leads to
disorientation, disconnection,
and Isolation.

Laws must be consistent with
the Truth to be legitimate.

Earth is a school and you submit your dissertation when you die.

It's about access, not replication.

Symbolic abstraction of
intelligence "Δ∞O" is
complete
and consistent.

# Infinitesimal($\Delta$ ) - Infinite($\infty$) - Finite(O).

# Complete(Δ) - Infinite(∞)-
# Incomplete(O).

# Consistent(Δ) - Infinite(∞)- Inconsistent(O).

# Time Complexity(Δ)-
# Dimensional Complexity(∞)-
# Space Complexity(O).

An
optimally efficient algorithm
has zero Time complexity($\Delta$),
zero Space complexity(O), and
an Infinite Dimensional
Complexity($\infty$).

Algorithmic efficiency can be more completely determined by not only accounting for the complexity of the computation that an algorithm carries out but also the complexity of the algorithm itself.

Space complexity(O) denotes the space required for execution, and Time complexity($\Delta$) denotes the number of operations required to complete execution.

Time complexity is measured by the
number of iterations it takes
for an algorithm to execute,
and Space complexity is
measured by
the amount of memory or
space required for the
algorithm to execute.

Finitary
algorithms have dimensional
complexities that are less than
infinite.

Incompleteness is a
fundamental property of
finitary algorithms.

Δ denotes Time complexity ∞ denotes
Dimensional complexity and O denotes Space complexity. Δ connotes infinitesimal and denotes Time complexity. ∞ connotes infinity and denotes Dimensional complexity. O connotes finite and denotes Space complexity.

The finite system is discrete
and the infinite system is
continuous.

The fundamental
representation
$\Delta\infty$O acts as a
conduit to General
Intelligence.

# Intelligence

Infinitesimal  Infinite   Finite

Complete   Infinite  Incomplete

Consistent   Infinite  Inconsistent

Time  Dimension  Space

Alexander Odilon Ngu          UnifiedIntelligence.DAO

## THE INTELLIGENCE
## STANDARD

**Δ∞O**
**[**
**Infinitesimal: "Δ"**
**Infinite: "∞"**
**Finite: "O"**
**]**

Alexander Odilon Ngu          UnifiedIntelligence.DAO

# The Language of Intelligence

### Alexander Ngu

| Infinitesimal | Infinite | Finite |
|---|---|---|
| Complete | Infinite | Incomplete |
| Consistent | Infinite | Inconsistent |
| Time Complexity | Dimensional Complexity | Space Complexity |
| $\omega()\Omega()$ | $\Delta \infty O$ | $O()o()$ |
| $<$ $<=$ | $\approx$ $=$ | $>=$ $>$ |

Universal Journal Of Intelligence          UnifiedIntelligence DAO

# V

## AFTERWORD

*The Man Who Killed The Equal Sign* is a compilation of Quotations, Questions, and Abstractions including, " The Death of the Equal sign defines the birth of new civilization". This collection culled from a few years of notes offers insight into Alexander Ngu's thoughts and unique perspective while on his journey to discovery. Overall, this work is aimed at challenging traditional ways of thinking and encouraging readers to think critically about the world around them.

# VI

## RESOURCES

Ngu, A. (2021). Dimensional Complexity and Algorithmic Efficiency.

Ngu, A. (2022). The Language of Intelligence.

Ngu, A. (2022). The Intelligence Black Paper.

# VII

## ABOUT THE AUTHOR

Amaya Odilon Kosso also known as Alexander Ngu also known as Amaya Odilon Ngu is a Cameroonian-American polymath, philosopher, and founder. His interests are diverse and encompass various domains, including Philosophy, Economics, Mathematics, Design, and the Arts. Amaya Odilon Kosso also known as Alexander Ngu discovered a law of nature, formulated a definition of intelligence, and introduced a new language and knowledge system. He is also known as *The Man Who Killed The Equal Sign*.

CHIEF AMAYA ODILON KOSSO
CHIEF ODILON KOSSO

# The Man Who Killed The Equal Sign

The Man Who Killed The Equal Sign